M000317442

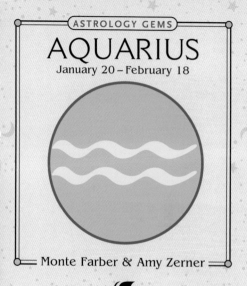

ASTROLOGY GEMS

# AQUARIUS

## January 20 – February 18

Monte Farber & Amy Zerner

Sterling Publishing Co., Inc.
New York

Text © 2006 by Monte Farber
Art © 2006 by Amy Zerner

10 9 8 7 6 5 4 3 2 1

Published by Sterling Publishing Co., Inc.
387 Park Avenue South, New York, NY 10016

Distributed in Canada by Sterling Publishing
c/o Canadian Manda Group, 165 Dufferin Street
Toronto, Ontario, Canada M6K 3H6

Distributed in the United Kingdom by GMC
Distribution Services
Castle Place, 166 High Street, Lewes, East Sussex,
England BN7 1XU

Distributed in Australia by Capricorn Link (Australia)
Pty. Ltd.
P.O. Box 704, Windsor, NSW 2756, Australia

Printed in China

Sterling ISBN-13: 978-1-4027-4175-3
           ISBN-10: 1-4027-4175-8

For information about custom editions, special sales,
premium and corporate purchases, please contact
Sterling Special Sales at 800-805-5489 or
specialsales@sterlingpub.com.

# What's Your Sign?

When someone asks you "What's your sign?" you know what that person really means is "What's your astrological sign?" Professional astrologers more often use the phrase "Sun sign," a term reflecting the concept that a person's sign is determined by which of the twelve signs of the zodiac the Sun appeared to be passing through at the moment she was born. The zodiac is the narrow band of sky circling the Earth's equator through which the Sun, the Moon, and the planets appear to move when viewed by us here on Earth.

# Astrology's Gift

Astrology, which has been around for thousands of years, is the study of how planetary positions relate to earthly events and people. Its long and rich history has resulted in a wealth of philosophical and psychological wisdom, the basic concepts of which we are going to share with you in the pages of this book. As the Greek philosopher Heracleitus (c. 540–c. 480 BCE) said, "Character is destiny." Who you are—complete with all of your goals, tendencies, habits, virtues, and vices—will

determine how you act and react, thereby creating your life's destiny. Like astrology itself, our Astrology Gems series is designed to help you to better know yourself and those you care about. You will then be better able to use your free will to shape your life to your liking.

# Does Astrology Work?

Many people rightly question how astrology can divide humanity into twelve Sun signs and make predictions that can be correct for everyone of the same sign. The simple answer is that it cannot do that—that's newspaper astrology, entertaining but not the real thing. Rather, astrology can help you understand your strengths and weaknesses so that you can better accept yourself as you are and use your strengths to compensate for your weaknesses. Real astrology is designed to help you to become yourself fully.

Remember, virtually all the music in the history of Western music has been composed using variations of the same twelve notes. Similarly, the twelve Sun signs of astrology are basic themes rich with meaning that each of us expresses differently to create and respond to the unique opportunities and challenges of our life.

# AQUARIUS

## January 20–February 18

### Planet
Uranus

### Element
Air

### Quality
Fixed

### Day
Saturday

### Season
winter

### Colors
electric blue, sky blue, ultraviolet

## Plants
tiger lily, bird of paradise, parsley

## Perfume
lemon verbena

## Gemstones
rock crystal, fluorite, azurite,
lapis lazuli

## Metal
uranium

## Personal qualities
Unique, brilliant, inventive, articulate,
and tolerant

We call the following words "keywords" because they can help you unlock the core meaning of the astrological sign of Aquarius. Each keyword represents issues and ideas that are of supreme importance and prominence in the lives of people born with Aquarius as their Sun sign. You will usually find that every Aquarius embodies at least one of these keywords in the way he makes a living:

inventive mind · detachment

humanitarianism · idealism

radicalism · altruism · rebellion

technical proficiency · genius

eclecticism · progressivism

power to the people · futuristic

originality · chaos theory

free thinker · space travel

unusual · eccentricity

explosivity · rebel without a cause

excitability · surprise · electrify

upset · revolutionary · reform

liberated · UFO · the Internet

## Aquarius' Symbolic Meaning

The symbol of the sign Aquarius is the Water Bearer pouring out his bounty to quench the thirst of world. For this reason, many people mistakenly think Aquarius is a Water sign. Water was the element the ancient sages connected with the realm of emotion, empathy, and intuition. However, Aquarius is not a Water sign. The element associated with

Aquarius is Air, the realm of ideas. People born under Aquarius like to think in broad and theoretical terms and want to "pour out" their ideas to quench the intellectual thirst of the world. Being mistaken for a Water sign is a very significant clue to an important lesson for Aquarians. Water symbolizes emotions and empathy, and Aquarians are often perceived to be lacking in both.

Aquarians, concerned for the good of all, are inspired to invent solutions to society's problems. They are the mad scientists and absentminded professors of the zodiac. To do this requires a free-thinking mind, unfettered by tradition or fear of disturbing the status quo. Aquarians learn from the past to change what they find distasteful in the present, for by doing that they create the future they envision. The emotional detachment necessary to see society's problems clearly and to try to solve them makes Aquarians seem to lack empathy for individuals' hardships. Aquarians should examine the actions they plan to take to make sure they will not be hurtful to others, even if hurting others is not their intent.

Aquarius is one of the four Fixed Sun signs in astrology (the other three are Taurus, Leo, and Scorpio). Fixed signs are concentrated, stubborn, and persistent. They are the ones who provide the stability to see things through. Aquarius is also one of the three Air signs in astrology (the other two are Libra and Gemini). Air represents the mind, ideas, and the ability to think; Aquarian ideas may be unusual or even original, but once formed, they tend to remain fixed. Aquarians refuse to budge whenever an issue involves what they believe to be a matter of principle.

Once an Aquarian is finished thinking about a subject theoretically, she lets her scientific mind take a break and returns to the world of emotions. In fact, she can easily feel herself being overcome by feelings of empathy for those less fortunate. This is what inspires her in the first place to come up with solutions to society's urgent problems.

## Recognizing an Aquarius

Aquarians often have a distant, dreamy look in their eyes. At other times their gaze is darting and anxious. They are likely to be taller than average, often with a lanky build that gives them a shambling walk. If their coloring is light, they are likely to be sandy haired. Aquarians may have an attractive, almost classic profile. Even if they are dressed expensively, their clothes never seem to fit quite right.

## Aquarius' Typical Behavior and Personality Traits

* friendly and easygoing
* likes groups and organizations
* can be totally eccentric
* an intuitive thinker with a practical side
* has a wide variety of interests
* involved with humanitarian causes
* has a mind of his own

- detached at times

- has a very ethical, moral code

- attracted to the mystical and the occult

- seeks to develop ideas and communicate them

- has a wide circle of friends from all walks of life

- accepts the many differences among people

# What Makes an Aquarius Tick?

Aquarians are here to learn how to make real the future they can so easily see in their mind's eye! This is why their life does not provide them with as many opportunities as they would like to enjoy the freedom and other resources necessary to turn their innovative ideas into reality. In fact, they sometimes make such extreme changes that in their enthusiasm to get rid of the old ways they can destroy valuable things from the past that still have great usefulness.

# The Aquarius Personality Expressed Positively

At their best, Aquarians are brilliant and engaging people who make friends with individuals from all walks of life. Despite being broad-minded, an ideal Aquarius has fixed ideas and stays true to them, even while being tolerant of other people's lifestyles, beliefs, and habits. Aquarius is often happiest when alone, so she can devote single-minded attention to her pet projects.

## On a Positive Note

*Aquarians displaying the positive characteristics associated with their sign also tend to be:*

* inventive and original

* thoughtful and caring

* cooperative and dependable

* intensely interested in humanity

* strong supporters of political reforms

* independent thinkers

* loyal friends and advocates

* scientific and intelligent

* communicative

# The Aquarius Personality Expressed Negatively

Frustrated or unhappy Aquarians may be rather crotchety, melancholy, and eccentric. They can be emotionally cold people and find it hard to show affection even for those closest to them. Despite their brilliant intelligence, negative Aquarians can be set in their ways and ideas. In extreme cases, they may even become hermits, unwilling to have their opinions assailed by other people.

## Negative Traits

*Aquarians displaying the negative characteristics associated with their sign also tend to be:*

❄ unwilling to compromise

❄ fanatical and unpredictable

❄ stubborn and tactless

❄ preoccupied with curiosities and weird obsessions

❄ perverse, with eccentric habits

❄ surprisingly lacking in confidence

❄ likely to shake up the status quo

# Ask an Aquarian If…

Ask an Aquarian if you want a simple answer to a complex problem. It helps if your problem is not too emotionally based, but even if it is, an Aquarius will give it a try. The Aquarian mind is highly analytical and skilled at making quick assessments; turning a myriad of information into easy-to-follow directions is never difficult for the people of this sign. Also, if you don't get it the first time, an Aquarius never tires of explaining things, and never condescends.

# Aquarians As Friends

An Aquarius friend is a constant source of mental stimulation, information, and practical help. Aquarians make many friends but few confidantes. Aquarius likes a friend who has intellectual interests and enjoys the unusual and the radical. She rarely passes judgment on the ethical codes of friends. Aquarius is friendly to anyone and tends to regard any relationship as platonic. An Aquarius takes great interest in her friends' ideas and projects, and enjoys giving advice and creative input. If an Aquarius wants to have the kind of friendships she has always dreamed of, she must avoid letting her tendency to go to extremes cause her to imagine that she must make radical changes that are really too much to ask of herself and others—changes that are bound to be too difficult to maintain.

# Looking for Love

Getting involved with groups of people who have come together for a common goal will help an Aquarius find love. Aquarians can often find their soul mate through a circle of friends, or by getting involved with people who are in fraternal organizations, societies, clubs, trade unions, trade associations, environmental groups, political activist groups, chat rooms, theme cruises, tour groups, group therapy, and all other ways that people get together for mutual support. Going to a place established to help people meet potential partners is favored for this sign. Aquarians have a natural talent for turning their eyes on an individual and seeming to create the basis of a close relationship after only a few days, so long as there are shared opinions, ideas, and aims. An Aquarian may seek to combine love and activism, since she is likely to fall for an individual who is equally socially conscious and politically aware.

Going to completely different kinds of places to meet people—even places an Aquarian might previously have thought were too bizarre—and being open to new and different types of people, the exact opposites of the kind an Aquarius may have been associating with in the past, would be good ways to find love. It is not unusual for Aquarians to be brought together with a potential love interest through unusual circumstances, since the sign itself rules coincidences.

# Finding That Special Someone

People do not usually have to make sweeping, radical changes in their lives to bring in the love that they desire, especially the kind of extreme changes that an Aquarian would be willing to make without a second's thought. For Aquarius, radical change is usually less complicated than for other signs, simply because Aquarians don't choose to do things according to plan. Aquarians don't question if a love interest comes into their life; they just accept it as a blessing from the universe.

# First Dates

Because Aquarians are up for virtually anything at any time, a first date can be whatever they or their dates choose. Plans for a first date could range from activities as disparate as taking a ride on bumper cars, to an evening volunteering at a shelter or soup kitchen, to a night spent gambling at a private club. There really aren't any no-no's when it comes to taking out an Aquarius for the first time. Aquarians can enjoy themselves in any number of ways, so long as the person they are with is as open, accepting, and spontaneous as they are.

## Aquarius in Love

Aquarians attract the opposite sex by their friendly, open manner, though they sometimes may try to seem glamorously aloof. Aquarians can be afraid of a deeply emotional involvement but genuinely want a real friendship with their loved ones. An Aquarian guards her independence and could even enjoy a living-apart relationship. A partner who makes too many demands, becomes jealous, or tries to put limitations on Aquarius' freedom is sure to be dropped quite suddenly.

## Undying Love

Often, Aquarians don't get involved in a love relationship, believing that it will become the be-all and end-all to them. Alas, Aquarians may misread or even second-guess their own emotions. Once they are deeply in love, however, they understand that it was only fear that was holding them back. They may not commit in the typical or conventional way. They are not always comfortable showing the depth of their love through sentimental behavior, but they will profess it often with sincere words and kind deeds.

# Expectations in Love

Aquarians expect their personal freedom of movement and action to be respected. They need total understanding and tolerance of their eccentricities. Aquarians are completely loyal and faithful to their partners. They expect their partners to enjoy frequent visits from a wide variety of friends from every walk of life.

Both people in any relationship must feel free and independent. This may sound like a contradiction in terms, but people in successful relationships can tell you that they have actually found the freedom to be themselves fully through their relationships. Being true to herself is a spiritual quest for an independent Aquarian thinker. If a partner can be supportive of that goal, he will improve his relationship with an Aquarius. Nothing is more enjoyable for an Aquarius than to be appreciated for who she really is.

An Aquarian's life is filled with unexpected events that cause her, eventually, to feel liberated. These events disrupt the status quo in her life and the lives of those she loves. Every relationship can change for the better. That is what makes her so attractive in the first place.

# What Aquarians Look For

Aquarians do not look for someone who will support them in every way or someone they can support in the same manner. More than anything, they want an equal—a person who will walk beside them, rather than lead or follow. Aquarians don't necessarily look for a love interest who will agree with their rather radical opinions. They appreciate people who have strong convictions of their own and who follow their own paths. Aquarians know that the better the friendship is, the better the love relationship will be.

# If Aquarians Only Knew...

If Aquarians only knew the deep love and affection their friends and others have for them, they would feel secure and not be worried about or take issue with emotional intimacy in their relationships. They would give themselves a chance to explore the ups and downs of emotional involvement without worrying that it would complicate life for them. Aquarians, once they open the floodgates, can come to terms with both past and present life events that have been awaiting resolution.

## Marriage

Once Aquarius has settled into a marriage, he does not like the idea of divorce and often wants to remain friends with a past partner. An Aquarian's relationships would benefit from actions calculated to improve his marriage. Joining, supporting, and advising a group or organization dedicated to relationships might strengthen an existing relationship or bring a new one into his life.

It is important to keep any relationship new and exciting. If Aquarius has done that, then his relationship is stronger than ever and ready for any unexpected challenges that might arise. If Aquarius has allowed things to get stuck at the same level with no growth or change, then he must get to work fixing it or his relationship will be tested by one or both partners acting rebelliously, out-of-the blue challenges, or both.

# Aquarius' Opposite Sign

Leo is the complementary opposite sign of Aquarius. Although relations between them can be difficult, Leo can show Aquarius how to make choices to please the self, rather than for an ideal. In this way, Aquarius can build emotional self-confidence. Also, the ease with which Leos handle their emotions can be a real eye-opener for Aquarians, who sometimes hide their true feelings under layers of logic and analytical assessments. In the same way, Aquarius can teach Leo self-control and intellectual discipline.

# Pairing Up

*In general, if people display the characteristics typical of their sign, intimate relationships between an Aquarius and another individual can be described as follows:*

## Aquarius with Aquarius

Harmonious, but represents a meeting of minds, not souls

## Aquarius with Pisces

Harmonious, if Aquarius will allow Pisces to be nurturing

## Aquarius with Aries

Harmonious; this pair makes a good business and romantic partnership

## Aquarius with Taurus
Difficult, unless Taurus allows Aquarius
the freedom she needs

## Aquarius with Gemini
Harmonious; a quirky and unique love
affair with great conversations

## Aquarius with Cancer
Turbulent but exciting, with lots of
sexual magnetism

## Aquarius with Leo
Difficult yet electric; a pair who fight in
public, make up in private

## Aquarius with Virgo
Turbulent, since they have almost
nothing in common but love

## Aquarius with Libra
Harmonious; a perfect pair: soul mates, lovers, and friends

## Aquarius with Scorpio
Difficult yet profound; a relationship arranged by destiny

## Aquarius with Sagittarius
Harmonious; completely in tune with each other's wants and needs

## Aquarius with Capricorn
Harmonious, with difficult patches; a karmic connection

# If Things Don't Work Out

If Aquarius wants out and a partner doesn't take the hint, Aquarius is fully capable of doing something to make the partner end the relationship. If the situation is reversed and Aquarius is left in the lurch, there is sure to be a period of emotional mourning, but after that he is ready to move on. Aquarius has way of always looking at life and events from a logical perspective, even when it involves love.

## Aquarius at Work

There is a tendency in just about every Aquarian to make work the center of her life. Her sense of dedication to what she does is considerable, and it can be difficult for even the most loving spouse or caring family member or friend to pry her away from it. But those who love Aquarius should understand that to expect anything but 100 percent total dedication from her is unrealistic.

As long as Aquarians feel that the work being done is important, they don't give a great deal of thought to where they stand in the overall chain of command. They can manage to show leadership without being the actual leader, and because they work well alone or with others, they rarely clash with those working above or below them.

They may not give the impression of great efficiency, but Aquarians have a unique ability to organize facts and relate them with amazing clarity. Their talent for communication puts them in a class by themselves, and because they have such dedication to what they are doing, they never leave a job undone.

# Typical Occupations

Aquarius can benefit from an investigation, analysis, innovation, or original idea. Scientist, astrologer, singer, charity worker, inventor, archeologist, radiographer, engineer, and humanitarian aid worker are all good career choices for an Aquarius. Working for groups that have organized for a common goal is favored. Some examples are trade unions and associations, fraternal organizations, credit unions, Internet chat rooms and the like, political groups, and environmental causes.

Aquarians work best on group projects. They make excellent researchers and admirable scientists, especially astronomers and natural historians. They may lead the field in photography, computer technology, or electronics. Aviation is also a natural vocation for Aquarians.

Aquarians' progressive talents are expressed well in writing and in broadcast television or radio presenter or writer. In the theater, they make good character actors and are natural mimics. Many Aquarians make fine and progressive musicians. They make effective welfare workers or educators.

## Details, Details

Aquarians don't think of themselves as detail-oriented people, and for the most part, they aren't. But that is mostly by choice. Actually, they have a fine mind for handling details, and they are particularly proficient at delegating detailed work to others, while still keeping an eye on all the areas and endeavors that comprise a project. Probably their best instinct for detailed work is being able to translate numbers and facts into concepts.

One reason Aquarians may not feel comfortable handling details is their tendency to be somewhat absentminded.

Their answer to this problem is to be nearly obsessive about writing things down. By keeping copious lists of facts, dates, times, and names, they are better able to manage projects that call for these things to be remembered. In this way, though Aquarians may worry quite a lot about keeping all their facts straight, they are probably better prepared than most people to handle them.

# Behavior and Abilities at Work

*In the workplace, a typical Aquarius:*

- dislikes routine and decision making
- likes to solve problems
- enjoys variety
- prefers mental to physical work
- enjoys working with a group
- has a good reputation among peers
- likes to work on her own

# Aquarius As Employer

*A typical Aquarius boss:*

- is quick thinking and a shrewd analyst

- is receptive to new ideas

- does not play favorites

- dislikes workplace cliques

- is full of surprising talents

- shows generosity to those doing special work

- gives employees fair compensation

- does not forgive lies or broken promises

- keeps promises

# Aquarius As Employee

*A typical Aquarius employee:*

- is aloof but gets along with most types

- is good at conceptualizing possibilities

- comes up with innovative ideas

- brings a fresh approach to any task

- frequently changes her job

- has great creative and analytical skills

- has leadership potential

## Aquarius As Coworker

The typical Aquarian is a loner, despite having a lot of workplace-based friendships. But he has the attributes of an Air sign—being able to get along with many different kinds of people without difficulty. Aquarius works well in groups, as team leader, or as a subordinate.

# Money

If an Aquarian comes up with an idea that she thinks can be sold, she should pursue it. Patent attorneys and venture capitalists may be receptive, especially to ideas for making people's lives better and longer and businesses more productive.

Computers and electronics are also favored moneymakers for Aquarians. A futuristic technology could be easy for an Aquarian to understand and profit from. Good fortune is more likely to come to an Aquarius through friends than through other ways. They may bring good fortune in the form of a gift or helpful advice.

Aquarians have a love/hate relationship with money. They love it for the freedom it brings but they hate the fact that they only have so much of it and are therefore restricted by it. Aquarians are drawn to charitable causes and are often the anonymous donors of substantial amounts.

## At Home

Aquarians can get so comfortable in their own home and their own space that they don't want to leave, which is one of the reasons many Aquarians work from home. But whether they do or not, they are at ease with an unconventional household schedule.

## Behavior and Abilities at Home

*Aquarius typically:*

- enjoys high-tech TVs and sound equipment

- lives in an unusually decorated space

- has a diverse group of houseguests

- fills her home with oddities

- eats strange mixtures of food and drink

- uses many tools, gizmos, and gear

- collects interesting photos and art

- takes unconventional vitamins and supplements

## Leisure Interests

While a great many of Aquarius' interests are intellectual, they also love tinkering with things, using their inventive skills to fix, create, or supplement technical gadgets or useful implements. Aquarians often work on several hobbies or interests at the same time.

*The typical Aquarius enjoys the following pastimes:*

* radical politics

* music, rhythm, and singing

* science fiction

* controlled exercise

* writing his personal journal

* scientific or inventive hobbies

* theater, comedy, and home movies

* flying, gliding, and parachuting

## Aquarian Likes

* fame or recognition

* learning about the world

* quiet time to think

* dreams and mystical experiences

* surprises and brilliant ideas

* the latest techno gadgets

* telling others what they think

* eccentric friends

* studying history

* travel to exotic places

## Aquarian Dislikes

* too much emotion
* people who are boring
* being taken for granted
* having freedom curtailed
* any kind of rip-off
* false advertising
* making loans or borrowing
* conformity
* revealing her own motives
* the herd mentality

# The Secret Side of Aquarius

Inside anyone who has strong Aquarian influences is a person who is extremely uncertain of his true identity. The Aquarius ego is the most precarious in the zodiac, because it is the sign of non-conformity. Intellectual genius, practical eccentricity, and mental oddity are all linked with Aquarius. The Aquarius personality has a powerful intellect. Putting this brainpower to good, practical use is the best way for Aquarius to build his ego.

# Uranus ♅

Uranus is the planet of eccentricity, genius, rebelliousness, revolution, and invention. It represents the forces in life that want to keep things new, exciting, and on the edge. It symbolizes the crisis of middle age that occurs at age forty, when people are tested to see whether they have made their lives a statement of their unique individuality. Uranus rules electricity and electrical devices such as computers, radios, and television sets, dynamite and all explosives, and especially futuristic devices. Uranus is the exposure to new ways of doing, making, and trying out inventions. A calm environment is essential to young Aquarius, because she is so sensitive to underlying tensions in the home. In practical terms, she needs to be taught simple methods for remembering things and for communicating her ideas to others.

Like any child, Aquarius needs love, especially in the form of respect, listening, appreciation, and friendship. Young Aquarius tends to act detached and dispassionate, sometimes finding close, intimate relationships difficult. She often looks more confident and acts older than she actually is, so parental encouragement and genuine interest in her ideas and needs should be expressed to reassure her.

# Aquarius As a Parent

*The typical Aquarius parent:*

* makes rational judgments

* is energetic and intelligent

* endorses modern educational theories

* does not overdiscipline or inhibit

* is prepared to discuss any problem

* encourages independence of thought

* does not like convention or conformity

* is a devoted friend for life

# The Aquarius Child

*The typical Aquarius child:*

- ❄ tends to be forgetful
- ❄ is sensitive and intuitive
- ❄ has unpredictable moods
- ❄ possesses amazing talents
- ❄ finds everything and everyone interesting
- ❄ is generous and kind to friends

- can have sudden outbursts of temper
- rebels against rules and regulations
- has lots of friends
- is very bright and grasps ideas quickly

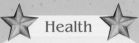

# Health

Aquarians have vast amounts of energy but often drive themselves into the ground, not knowing when they are tired. They have the habit of not listening to others' advice to slow down, and they can be rebellious patients who won't admit defeat. Aquarians need lots of fresh air, plenty of sleep, and regular exercise to stay healthy. Often, their work puts great demands on their eyesight and their time, but they should never miss an appointment at the optician's. They can have poor circulation, manifesting itself in leg and ankle problems, which are the body parts that Aquarius rules.

# ⭐ Famous Aquarians ⭐

**Jennifer Aniston**

Mikhail Baryshnikov

**Garth Brooks**

Sheryl Crow

**James Dean**

Charles Dickens

**Christian Dior**

Thomas Edison

**Mia Farrow**

Clark Gable

**Michael Jordan**

Abraham Lincoln

**Charles Lindbergh**

Wolfgang Amadeus Mozart

**Paul Newman**

Yoko Ono

**Lisa Marie Presley**

Ronald Reagan

**Christina Ricci**

Franklin Delano Roosevelt

**Babe Ruth**

John Travolta

**Lana Turner**

Oprah Winfrey

**Virginia Woolf**

THE ENCHANTED WORLD of AMY ZERNER & MONTE FARBER

# About the Authors

Internationally known self-help author Monte Farber's inspiring guidance and empathic insights impact everyone he encounters. Amy Zerner's exquisite one-of-a-kind spiritual couture creations and collaged fabric paintings exude her profound intuition and deep connection with archetypal stories and healing energies. Together, they have built The Enchanted World of Amy Zerner and Monte Farber: books, card decks, and

oracles that have helped millions discover their own spiritual paths.

Their best-selling titles include The Chakra Meditation Kit, The Enchanted Tarot, The Instant Tarot Reader, The Psychic Circle, Karma Cards, The Truth Fairy, The Healing Deck, True Love Tarot, Animal Powers Meditation Kit, The Breathe Easy Deck, The Pathfinder Psychic Talking Board, and Gifts of the Goddess Affirmation Cards.

For further information, please visit: **www.TheEnchantedWorld.com**